FUN
in the
SUN

JIM DAVIS

RAVETTE PUBLISHING

First published by Ravette Publishing 2001

Printed and bound in Great Britain
for Ravette Publishing Limited,
Unit 3, Tristar Centre,
Star Road, Partridge Green,
West Sussex RH13 8RA
by Cox & Wyman Ltd, Reading, Berkshire

ISBN: 1 84161 097 6

I STARTED WITHOUT YOU

JIM DAVIS 3-18

JIM DAVIS 4-24

I HAVE BOTH ARMS IN THE SAME SLEEVE

I THINK IT'S BEST TO KEEP WALKING

JIM DAVIS 6-12

OTHER GARFIELD BOOKS AVAILABLE

Pocket Books	Price	ISBN
Bon Appetit	£3.50	1 84161 038 0
Byte Me	£3.50	1 84161 009 7
Double Trouble	£3.50	1 84161 008 9
A Gift For You	£3.50	1 85304 190 4
The Gladiator	£3.50	1 85304 941 7
Gooooooal!	£3.50	1 84161 037 2
Great Impressions	£3.50	1 85304 191 2
Hangs On	£2.99	1 85304 784 8
Here We Go Again	£2.99	0 948456 10 8
In Training	£3.50	1 85304 785 6
The Irresistible	£3.50	1 85304 940 9
Le Magnifique!	£3.50	1 85304 243 9
Let's Party	£3.50	1 85304 906 9
Light Of My Life	£3.50	1 85304 353 2
On The Right Track	£3.50	1 85304 907 7
Pick Of The Bunch	£2.99	1 85304 258 7
Says It With Flowers	£2.99	1 85304 316 8
Shove At First Sight	£3.50	1 85304 990 5
To Eat Or Not To Eat?	£3.50	1 85304 991 3
Wave Rebel	£3.50	1 85304 317 6
With Love From Me To You	£3.50	1 85304 392 3

new title available Feb 2002:

No. 44 - Eat My Dust	£3.50	1 84161 098 4

Theme Books		
Guide to Behaving Badly	£4.50	1 85304 892 5
Guide to Being a Couch Potato	£3.99	1 84161 039 9
Guide to Creatures Great & Small	£3.99	1 85304 998 0
Guide to Friends	£3.99	1 84161 040 2
Guide to Healthy Living	£3.99	1 85304 972 7
Guide to Insults	£3.99	1 85304 895 X
Guide to Pigging Out	£4.50	1 85304 893 3
Guide to Romance	£3.99	1 85304 894 1
Guide to The Seasons	£3.99	1 85304 999 9
Guide to Successful Living	£3.99	1 85304 973 5

new titles now available:

Guide to Coffee Mornings	£4.50	1 84161 086 0
Guide to Cat Napping	£4.50	1 84161 087 9

Classics	Price	ISBN
Volume One	£4.99	1 85304 970 0
Volume Two	£5.99	1 85304 971 9
Volume Three	£5.99	1 85304 996 4
Volume Four	£5.99	1 85304 997 2
Volume Five	£4.99	1 84161 022 4
Volume Six	£5.99	1 84161 023 2

new titles now available:

Volume Seven	£5.99	1 84161 088 7
Volume Eight	£5.99	1 84161 089 5

Miscellaneous

new title now available

Garfield Treasury 2	£9.99	1 84161 042 9
Garfield Address Book (indexed)	£4.99 inc VAT	1 85304 904 2
Garfield 21st Birthday Celebration Book	£9.99	1 85304 995 6

All Garfield books are available at your local bookshop or from the address below. Just tick the titles required and send the form with your payment to:-

BBCS, P O Box 941, Kingston upon Hull HU1 3YQ
24-hour telephone credit card line 01482 224626
Prices and availability are subject to change without notice.
Please enclose a cheque or postal order made payable to BBCS to the value of the cover price of the book and allow the following for postage and packing:

UK & BFPO:	£1.95 (weight up to 1kg)	3-day delivery
	£2.95 (weight over 1kg up to 20kg)	3-day delivery
	£4.95 (weight up to 20kg)	next day delivery

EU & Eire:	Surface Mail	£2.50 for first book & £1.50 for subsequent books
	Airmail	£4.00 for first book & £2.50 for subsequent books
USA:	Surface Mail	£4.50 for first book & £2.50 for subsequent books
	Airmail	£7.50 for first book & £3.50 for subsequent books
Rest of the World:	Surface Mail	£6.00 for first book & £3.50 for subsequent books
	Airmail	£10.00 for first book & £4.50 for subsequent books

Name ....

Address ....

....

....

Cards accepted: Visa, Mastercard, Switch, Delta, American Express

☐☐☐☐☐☐☐☐☐☐☐☐☐☐☐☐☐☐

Expiry Date.......................Signature ....